Watch Me Rise: Recipes for bread, Poems
for growth
By Dayna Altman

Acknowledgements

A huge thank you to all who helped to make this book come to life.

Jason SonDu Taglieri, my partner in all things design, publishing and producing Bake it Till You Make it. I am eternally grateful for your dedication and expertise. Your support of this brand has allowed me to make anything and everything possible.

Brenna Stewart, thank you for adding the elements of photography to this book. Every single Bake it Till You Make it book has a bit of you in it and that means so much to me.

To all of the people in my life who have continued to push me to share my poetry although it still feels a little outside of my comfort zone. Thank you for brainstorming, reviewing and supporting each poem.

Sam, this is a success for both of us. Your unconditional love has helped me believe I can do anything!

Last but not least a huge thank you to all who illustrated this book, both in the Bake it Till You Make it LLC community and in my own network and personal community. Seeing the art you created emerge from my words has been a magical experience.

And on that note, a VERY special thank you and acknowledgement to the four humans who have seen this project from the beginning: Gabriela Alvarez, Mekkailah Chourb, Iwinosa Foster-Efosa and Elvira Tejada-Lemus. Thank you for believing in my work and finding your own ways to express it through illustrating the majority of this book. Each of you are so incredibly talented in your own way and the four of you have changed me for the better; that is a gift I would not trade for anything.

Dedication

Dedicated to all who have not felt at home
in their bodies or within themselves. For
those who do not know what their next step
is, for those who feel alone or stuck in
shame: you do not have to hide, you are seen
and you are important. You are already
home, you will rise.

Trigger Warning

This book explores themes related to mental
illness and sexual violence. Please advise as
these topics are difficult for many. While
this collection of poems is written with hope
and empowerment in mind, some poems
explore the painful journey to find it. If you
are in crisis and need immediate assistance,
please call the National Suicide Prevention
Lifeline by dialing 988 or text HOME to
741-741 to reach the Crisis Textline.

Table of Contents

Preface

Am I enough? Is what I am doing enough?

These are the questions that have kept me up at night since I was in elementary school and now 20 years later, I still look at the ceiling at 1AM and wonder the same thing. My mental health journey, my life's journey for that matter, has oftentimes been derailed and sabotaged when my answer to these questions is "no."

I have often thought about where this doubt and constant questioning of myself comes from. Certainly the environment I grew up in; despite the immense privilege that came with growing up in Southboro Massachusetts, aka an affluent town with an abundance of resources; I felt if I had everything at my disposal, there was no reason I should not be "perfect". Perfect to me meant: flawless, pleasing, lovely, adorable, someone who never made a mistake; it was the only way I thought I would be loved. I felt this was the only way I could move throughout the world and it has taken me years to untangle my innate worth as a human from the one I thought I had to prove and earn (still working on it!) I am happy to say that at this point in my life, I consider myself a recovering perfectionist. This has coincided with the work I have done in long term eating disorder recovery as well as learning to manage, navigate and live with anxiety fueled OCD and major depressive disorder. A true turning point for me on this journey of feeling as though I am enough, has been through my mental health advocacy specifically Bake it Till You Make it. Bake it Till You Make it: is the community based LLC that I solely run and operate to inspire mental health conversation in the kitchen, around the table and beyond. It is through this organization, I have leaned into being an authentic leader. One who still struggles with her mental health and baking things without forgetting to put the eggs in or leaving the kitchen floor a mess of sprinkles.

As my therapist Dena once said, I have been "vulnerable before it was trendy" and I plan to continue to do just that.

So why start this book of poems with an essay like this one? Well, when I was getting ready to put the final touches on the manuscript, this narrative about "enough-ness" came up. Is it long enough? Is it good enough? I am still learning how to craft poetry, is what I am putting out into the world enough?

I have often felt that if I just had validation that I was enough that would solve every insecurity. For years, I thought it would come from my parents, my sister, a partner, someone I looked up to, a therapist etc. but I have come to recognize the only person that will ever be able to answer this question is me. As I shuffled through these pages looking for where I could add a few more words or poems or recipes for optimal "enoughness", I was quickly reminded that this battle would not be won by adding 100 more pages, it would only be won when I started to accept myself.

So how did I decide this book was enough to get into your hands as the reader? Well I am not totally sure I know, because I still feel insecure about it. However, I know leading with vulnerability has propelled me into living a life that I am proud of, so I am not going to let that stop me. Plus, I am not sure when this would ever feel enough and I truly believe these poems need to be read and felt, these messages need to be heard.

So here I am and here you are.

I hope wherever you are right now this book is finding you at the right time. Whether you are here
because you are curious about the way a poetry book could follow the arc of a recipe or you are in need of inspiration, you are welcome.

I decided to begin not only with this essay but also an accompanying poem I wrote entitled "Scattered." I think so much of my feelings of inadequacy come from feeling as though I don't have a clear direction. And how could someone who is "scattered" feel enough as they are?

So, in Dayna fashion, I decided to turn this idea on its head. I have reclaimed scattered, I am empowered by scattered, we are all scattered and we all still belong.

———----

Scattered

I exist not in one place
But in thousands
There are pieces of me everywhere
And yet my whole life, I have wondered where I fit.

My tears have touched surfaces
That know, no bounds

Every coffee shop napkin I have crumpled
Every seat belt buckled
On a train, car
Or plane,
Every time I have fallen and picked up
myself up again,
I am scattered.

Every microphone I have touched,
To tell my story,
The words I have heard,
the ones I have said,
The ones repurposed as platforms
To talk about things that matter.
The things that harm us that we can't see,
Things that scare us,
The things that we can't control.
I feel most alive on those stages
And in those spaces,
Where my words illustrate the mosaic of
experiences that
Silenced me.
The years of
doubting my worth
And fighting for a place on this earth,

This mosaic is now a window, for others like
me
One where we can clearly see it was never
really
About fitting in.

For every person that doubted you
Every experience that scarred you,
That left you wondering where you fit,
You exist not in one places but in thousands
And in every place,
You belong.

Assemble (verb): to bring together (as in a particular place or for a particular purpose)

1. *I assemble the ingredients for the bread I will make.*

2. *I assemble the memories and the moments that have gotten me here.*

II.

perception

I am alone
In the way I perceive the world
The lens of my kaleidoscope
seems to be tighter than most
My big emotions
Bust open the bounds of my scope
The vibrant colors
fill in the lines
Of this black and white world.

When I zoom in,
I can barely see anything
But color,
No shapes or silhouettes
Allow for perspective
I can't zoom out
I am left in the oranges
Blues and greens
Of feeling
No boundaries
Or ways to rein in
The way I am feeling
For years I felt my kaleidoscope

Was broken.

Years of befriending these colors
Has allowed me to see
That vibrancy is powerful
Boundaries are what reins in
The scope
Despite the pain
They can cause at first
It's the only way my perception will work
And fit
Into a world not made of color but
For those who see in black and white.

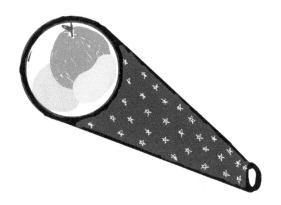

Sit Tight

Sitting still is near impossible
With an anxious brain.
The thoughts
Overflowing
Like bubbles in a bath
Don't allow me to enjoy this moment
Of "self care"
It becomes self
Sabotage.

Now it's about what I am not doing
While I am sitting still
Not moving
Not working
Not breathing

Now
As I make a never ending to-do list
When I am supposed to be sitting still?
Maybe I will write
Or maybe I will reflect,
As much as I want to forget
The pain

That I face
Comes completely from within
I wonder how I will make it out
If I can't connect in.

Homesick

I am homesick for a place that does not exist
A crisp air at my back
As I open the door to a house full of warmth
A place filled with so much kindness,
It's like I understand the word "gentle"
In a way I never thought was possible.

I have many homes.
I guess that makes me lucky,
Homes with lavish rooms
And big garage doors
Homes with views so vast
It's as if I am on top of the world,
If money could buy the place I am longing
for
I would already have it.

That's the thing
This cannot be bought
Or sold
There is only one and it belongs to me
It is the house in which my soul lives
But I don't feel at home there

The damage I have done to a place
That just wants to keep me safe
Makes it hard to feel at home in what binds
my body
I have a home
I am homesick for a feeling,
Tolerance,
Trust,
Acceptance.

Crossroads

I am at a crossroads
Stuck at the intersection
Of recovery
And one missed step
Where a slip
Becomes a slide
Becomes a sleepless night
Starving
Tossing, turning
Becomes a dip into a need for validation
The "did you lose weight" or
The "you look so good"
These comments turn me into
A shell of a person,
One who only knows her
Eating Disorder.

I know the direction in which I choose to
step
Will determine my future
A pros and cons list
Doesn't seem to do justice
For a decision that feels impossible.

I am
driving blindly the wrong way

Down a one way
I wish I knew the right way
Where do I go from here?

Lost and Found

Healing will happen on Hope Avenue
Between the neighborhood of 2 bedroom
apartments
And an open tennis court, sat the place
where "I would get my life back"
If only I knew eating disorder treatment was
40 minutes away,
I would have gotten in my car to get here
years ago.
I came for healing here,
6 weeks later,
I couldn't find it.

I looked for healing in Kathy's office.
On the hottest days of summer,
My tears stuck to her leather couch.
The weight of my hopeless heart in therapy
never allowed me
To get comfortable on that leather.

I thought healing was supposed to be
comfortable,
So, I definitely wouldn't find it on this
couch.

Healing was promised to me on the other
side of 2012.
The year in which I had been hospitalized
for my mental health
More times than I would like to admit.
I believed I would find healing embedded in
the messages of my "goodbye book"
Or hidden in the pockets of the sweatshirts
that were returned to me during discharge.
Healing, I can't find you.

Healing, where are you?
I am broken.
The work that I put into recovery all of these
years prior has been completely erased.
Every step I took, every moment, I felt
closer to you is no longer familiar to me,
I don't know how I am supposed to believe
you exist
When I was sexually assaulted on a trip
abroad to find God.

Healing I am ready, I am a college graduate!
The full circle moment you have been
waiting to surprise me for,
is here.
I am a survivor,
I am in recovery,

Healing,
I am in disbelief, I didn't find you
On the back of my diploma.
I thought healing and accomplishment were
the same thing.

Healing this is getting old.
I am almost 30 and I am kind of impressive
now *(if I do say so myself)*
I am checking "the boxes",
I have a costco membership,
I host dinner parties,
I am making waves in the world,
I create things that help people,
I am finding myself,
And yet you still feel out of reach.

–

Healing it has been years and I am still
trying to understand
But maybe you do not come in one moment
Maybe you were there all along.

Not a Role Model

My friend Lilly
takes a modeling class on Sundays
The instructor told her
If she wants to walk the runway
She needs to hit the gym for three
Hours a day
The only thing they are modeling for her
Is an eating disorder.
She is eleven.
No wonder why
We don't feel good enough.

Stress Hives

I am under attack
And I have no defense.
I am not equipped with armor,
I have no manual or map,
I keep repeating:
I am not ready,
I am not ready.
I am on high alert.

My immune system detects
An intruder
If only it knew this is an inside job.

You Do Not Have to Prove Yourself Banana Bread

The perfect recipe for when you are unsure of yourself. Adding chocolate chips to something traditional will help you realize you are made to stand out. This bread rises in the oven without time in a proving drawer: you don't have to prove yourself to anyone.

Ingredients

- 4 ripe bananas
- 1 ½ cups white sugar
- 1 egg
- ½ cup melted butter
- 1 ½ cups all purpose flour
- 1 teaspoon baking powder
- 1 teaspoon salt
- 1 cup chocolate chips

Equipment
- Loaf Pan

Directions

1. Preheat the oven to 325F and grease the loaf pan.
2. Mash four bananas thoroughly in a bowl.
3. Add sugar, the egg and butter together in the bowl with the bananas, stir.
4. In a separate bowl, mix flour, salt and baking powder together.
5. Stir flour and baking powder mixture into the banana mixture bowl, stir to combine but do not overmix.
6. Add one cup of chocolate chips, stir.
7. Pour batter into the loaf pan and bake in the oven for 50 minutes or

until a toothpick comes out clean in
the center of the bread.

8. Let cool and slice to enjoy.

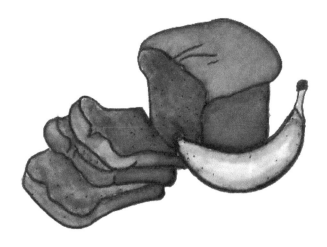

Dissolve (verb): become or cause to become incorporated into a liquid so as to form a solution.

1. *Let the yeast dissolve in water.*

2. *Living with mental illness, my mental health at times can deteriorate and dissolve.*

Held up

My mental illness robs me of the present
It holds me up.

It puts my life on the line
As I put my hands up.
I am in pain,
I feel
Everything.
For a moment,
I wonder what it is like to feel numb.
As someone who feels so deeply,
I question what it is like to be senseless
How does it feel
To feel nothing,
When you are being held up?

I am held up.
I hold onto nothing.
I am held up
I can't grasp reality
I am held up,
Nothing seems to matter anymore
It's hard to recover.

Skin

During the hardest times,
I shed a layer of emotional skin.
This is a dangerous way to live
When life's debris seems to fall from the sky
And crash down on me in an instant.

A broken relationship
An unfinished conversation
I replay it in my head
Until I can't make sense of why
I can't
Break the cycle
Or silence the loop.

I try to patch up my wounds
With what is left of me
With what I know best
But without a layer protection
I bleed with every move.

The skin grows back
Only when I look within
A difficult task
With no tools,
I don't know how to find my
own strength.

Time heals.
Therapy heals.
Skills heal.
Routine heals.
Structure heals.
Relationships heal.
I heal.
The skin slowly grows.

Starving

I don't want my existence to be about my
body
But it is hard for it not to be
When it is the subtext of every conversation.

It is hard to be hungry in this house
When I feel starved for an existence that
doesn't have to do with the way I look.

I hate my body.
I compare its every piece
I remember what it was like to not be so big
A smaller appetite
A smaller life
A smaller mind that only
Counted calories.

I feel like everywhere I go
I am searching for a comparable body That
maybe if I see my size on
Someone else
I won't feel that bad.
But is that all you see,
When you look at me:
A body?
What about my soul?

Silence

I have hit a new type of empty
Where I have nothing to say.

My heart twists in pain
While tears drip from my eyes
My chest is tight
breathing heavy
I try to form words to describe
This empty
But nothing leaves my lips.

Its as if a bottomless pit
Lies below my heart.
There is nothing to catch me,
There is no end to this empty
Silence.

Dark and Twisty Pretzels

A recipe for when things feel "dark and twisty". A term a dear friend of mine coined for when things feel out of control and depression takes over. Realizing I do not have control of anything is maybe the hardest thing I have had to accept and continue to accept each day. Sometimes embracing the pain and the "out of control-ness" is the only way to cope.

Ingredients

- 1 ½ cups warm water
- 1 packet of instant yeast
- 1 teaspoon salt
- 1 tablespoon brown sugar
- 1 ½ tablespoons unsalted butter, melted
- 4 cups all purpose flour
- Sea salt for sprinkling

Equipment

- 2 baking sheets
- Parchment paper
- Towel

Directions

1. Preheat the oven to 400F.
2. In a bowl, whisk the yeast into the warm water and set a timer for one minute, letting it sit.
3. After the minute, whisk in salt, brown sugar and melted butter.
4. Gradually add one cup of flour at a time into the bowl, mixing with a wooden spoon until dough becomes thick.
5. Turn dough out of the bowl and onto a floured surface, knead for three minutes and shape into a ball.
6. Cover the dough with a towel and allow it to rest for ten minutes.
7. Line two baking sheets with parchment paper and set aside.

8. After ten minutes have passed, cut the dough into three sections and roll the dough into a rope (about 2 feet).

9. Take the ends and draw them together to form a circle and twist them to create a pretzel shape.

10. Place pretzels on a baking sheet and sprinkle salt.

11. Bake for 14 minutes or until golden brown.

12. Serve warm.

100mg

I am desperate for a change
But it's hard to believe the pill
I am holding in the palm of my hand
Will make any type of difference
In the way I feel
Or don't feel
The flood
And numb
cycle makes it hard to decipher
What my brain is is actually trying to tell
me.

The relentless pain that comes with living
When I am deeply depressed makes it hard
to hold onto
Any type of hope
Especially if it comes in the form of a
100mg tablet
The side effects made it harder to
understand
If anything has changed,
My mind is incredibly powerful even when
it is working against me.

But maybe this neurological adjustment
Will help me recognize

That I am just trying my best
To put some "guardrails" on these emotions
That have no limits,
I am at my limit..
Maybe I will take this pill.

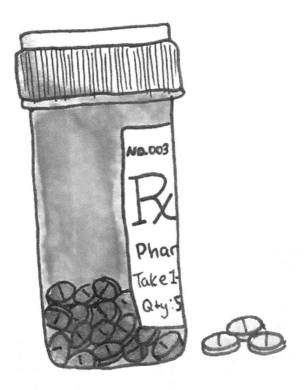

Anxiety

Panic strikes out of nowhere
And yet I refrain from calling a friend.
Learning to look inward for comfort is the
hardest thing I have done
In a long time.
I am scared.
It will subside.
It will subside.

(Not a) Friend

Being friends with you
is like being picked last in gym class
A convenient not so first choice.
I drop my phone,
as you hang up on the other line.
I mumble,
Why am I so hard to love?

This question leaves me doubting
every piece of my being.

I pull a part my identity
As if it as easy to dissect
a four leaf clover:
I feel like
The unluckiest girl
In the world.

Do you know what it is like to
Hold on to toxicity because it is
Easier than being alone?

Do you know what it is like to be your
friend?

19

I left school in late January
Right before midterms,
My parents thought that maybe removing
the burden of school
Would remove the depression,
It didn't work.

In February I got a job at the mall
Selling beauty products at a kiosk
As if marketing something to help the
exterior
Would heal my internal pain.

In March, I put on my pointe shoes
Believing the bleeding of my toes
Would mask the pain in my heart,
It still hurt.

I laid on the couch for hours
Convinced the combination of Disney
Channel
And my pink onesie
Would relieve my will to die.
I was only 19.

Each time I thought I hit rock bottom

I fell another one thousand feet.
Wondering how many more times it would take
Before the ground would open up beneath me
And swallow me whole

But there must have been a will to live
Because I am still here
My ground opens up beneath me
But with dirt on my hands,
I patch the soil together
To arrive on broken ground.

Do I like Gluten?: Gluten Free (No Knead) Bread

I eat (and love) things that contain gluten but for a long time, I had no idea who I was. What did I like and what did I dislike? Where did I begin and others end? Did I like gluten? This recipe is for those who are still figuring it out. Trial and error is sometimes the best place to start.

Ingredients

- 2 cups warm water
- 2 cups white sugar
- 1 packet active dry yeast
- ¼ cup ground chia seeds
- 1 cup brown rice flour
- ¾ cup oat flour
- 1 cup potato starch
- ¾ cup sorghum flour
- 2 teaspoons salt

<u>Equipment</u>

- 8 x 4 inch loaf pan
- Towel

<u>Instructions</u>

1. In a medium bowl, whisk water and sugar, then add the packet of yeast. Let it sit on the counter for 10 minutes.
2. Once the yeast has become frothy, whisk in chia seeds and let it sit for another 10 minutes, set aside.
3. In a large bowl, whisk together rice flour, oat flour, potato starch, sorghum flour and salt.
4. Add the wet ingredients to the center of the dry and stir with a wooden spoon.
5. Put the batter into the greased loaf pan and cover it with a towel to proof for an hour in a warm place.
6. Preheat the oven to 425F and bake for 45 minutes.

7. After 45 minutes, turn down the oven to 375 degrees for 30 minutes.
8. Remove the bread from the oven and let it cool before cutting into it, enjoy.

Knead (verb): work (moistened flour or clay) into dough or paste with the hand.

1. *I knead the dough before I set it aside to bake.*

2. *My life feels like a work in progress. I need to work through the hard parts before I set it aside; I knead.*

An ode to all things bad for me

I never give anything away.

Maybe it is my old soul
Or sentimental disposition
But I seldom part with anything I don't have
to.

My childhood bedroom remains untouched.
My stuffed animals line
The perimeter of my bed
Beside a pile of journals
That tell the stories of my eighth grade
isolation.

I have held onto every holiday card
And birthday candle,
I do not let go.

That is why
Giving you away feels impossible.

My comfort
My illness.

You distract me from shame,
You are the answers to my unsolved crisis

You protect me from life
But you do not let me live it.

I don't know how to give you away.

My brain

It is here I collect.
I search,
I gather,
I build.
I string together my coping skills
As if they are the beads on a bracelet
If only it was as easy
To use a skill
As it is to fidget
With a piece of plastic on my wrist.
I guess there are many forms
Of distraction

I make phone calls
I write poems
I see my therapist,
Sometimes more than once
A week

I make art,
I cry
I grieve
I rebuild
I always rebuild.

Why I am afraid to be a beginner at anything: Sourdough Starter Recipe for Beginners

The pressure I have put on myself throughout my life has been insurmountable; I have had to be good at everything. It is as if being a beginner at anything was something to be embarrassed about. I have avoided things I love just because I have felt I am not good at them, but that isn't fair to anyone, especially me. I live a lot of my life afraid, but I don't think I have to always be afraid of something new.

Ingredients

- 4 cups bread flour
- 2 teaspoons salt
- 2 cups water
- ½ cup sourdough starter

Equipment
- Towel
- Loaf Pan

<u>Directions</u>

1. Begin the process by leaving out your sourdough starter on the counter for about eight hours.
2. Eight hours later, put flour in a medium bowl and add salt.
3. Mix starter and water in a small bowl, mix well.
4. Pour starter mixture into flour using a wooden spoon for about 2 minutes.
5. Cover with a towel and rest for 15 minutes.
6. After 15 minutes have passed, stretch out the dough from side to side and stretch it upward for about 45 seconds.
7. Cover and repeat the process 15 minutes later (three more times).
8. Proof overnight by covering the bowl with a damp towel.
9. About 12 hours later, the dough should have expanded.
10. Next, loosen the dough from the edges of a bowl with wet fingers.

Pull the dough straight up from the center.

11. After this first stretch, give the bowl a turn and wet your hands again after about 60 seconds, stretch it and fold it over in the bowl, do this three times.

12. Place the bowl in the refrigerator for one hour (uncovered).

13. Preheat the oven to 475F with a dutch oven inside.

14. When ready to bake, score dough with a sharp knife with one slit.

15. Place dutch oven in the middle at 475F for 30 minutes.

16. Let it cool for up to an hour and enjoy.

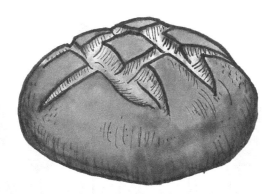

If ED could speak

If my body could speak
It would be crying out in pain.
The result of years of restricting
Has me counting down the minutes
until
the
meal
is
over.

The way I see food
As if it's some type of math equation
I count the calories in, only to plan
How to get them out.

But this isn't just about me and my body
It is about you and yours...

Congrats you win,
The race I feared I would always lose
The race to thin-ness
To be too small to ignore.
I lost it a long time ago.
Sometimes I wish I could go back.

My mind is my biggest blessing

And my greatest curse.
I want to exist beyond my body.
Sometimes I don't know how.

The Invisible War

You assume I hate my body
And sometimes you are not wrong
But the words that leave your lips,
cut deeper than you can imagine.
You throw salt in the
Invisible wounds that lie beneath what you
can see.
The wounds sustained
In the war against my body.

The ones from the dressing room,
The ones in the car,
The ones in the mirror.

My body is not your validator
Or means of conversation

I am not interested in hearing what you have
to say about the house I live in
Because
I never gave consent
To be involved in the competition you have
created
I don't want to be at war
Anymore
With you

But more than that
With my body

I surrender.

Duality

When you feel too much
You can empathize with anyone
Others feel safe with you because they see
you feeling too.
Gifts come in the form of presence
Because the best feeling happens in action
together.
When you feel too much
The big days are the best days
Feeling isn't finite like pizza
It's a well of endless activation that never
seems to end
I float in waves to the highest peaks of
emotion,
I feel it all.

When you feel too much
There is no bandage big enough for the
ache.
Whether it is a big one or small one
Nothing fits.
No gauze or tape

Will ever cover the oozing feeling that
becomes
insurmountable.

When you feel too much
You get scared all the time
That someone will find out
What is happening in your head
That you will be cast aside, labeled
Too much.
When you feel too much,
The hardest moments are the worst
moments.
I can't seem to ever find my raft as I paddle
back the waves
In the depths of being.

When you feel too much
You feel grateful
And shameful
All at once
You appreciate the gifts it brings
But tired by its curse.

Honor

Being brave doesn't always come with a
badge of honor
But I think it should.
Something shiny and gold
That professes to the world
I went out of my way to be uncomfortable.

But we don't celebrate that,
What a shame.

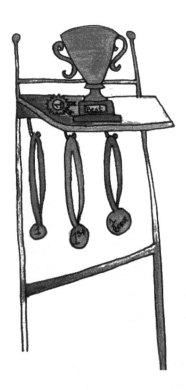

Magical thinking

The safety of my family
Weighs heavily on my shoulders
An unfathomable load
Overwhelms my muscles
I shake as I mutter
It is completely up to me.

Or that's what my OCD tells me
Three clicks of my car lock button
Or two turns to the right on the door
I have taught myself
It is the way I think about harm
That
Will predict the future.

I scan for patterns
As I pull the first layer of
Skin off my lips
If only I could peel back
And unpack
These disordered thoughts

When I see it on paper
Or hear it out loud
It sounds like some sort of God complex
If only it was

as complex
As a sense of entitlement
I feel entitled
To nothing but fear
That every thought must be free
Of words that could indicate danger
This magical thinking
Has stripped me of
My confidence
I can't trust anyone
Especially myself

My therapist says
These thoughts are just
Trying to protect me
But it's hard to imagine the uncertainty
That accompanies this sense of overwhelm
Has done anything but hurt me.
I need control
I can't live in the unknown
It feels impossible to quiet
The stream of solutions that
Flood my brain
I would like to believe
In this magic.

Freedom...?

It is not that you are afraid of sex
It's that you don't where the loves fits in
Is it between the bodies
Or under the sheets?
You don't understand how sex is supposed
to be joyful
With all the pain it has caused you.
You see it in movies
You read about it in magazines,
You don't get it.

It's not that you don't trust yourself
It's that you don't have an inner compass.
He smashed the glass that used to tell you if
you should stay
or run from a guy
Who you meet online or at a bar.
You still feel the shattered pieces in your
body
You wonder if it will stop stinging.

It is not that you don't want intimacy
It's that you didn't choose the first time.
You tuck away the fantasy of being believed
when they ask if
you were exaggerating in the first place.

It is not that you will feel like a victim
forever
There are some moments your survivorship
feels so overwhelming
You swear you are wearing a cape
But the tears you cry over feeling broken
will always be a reminder of the way
This world would rather shame survivors
than "ruin a young man's future"
You will continue to create, to fight, to
inspire...

It's not that you want this forever
It's that you wonder if you will ever feel
free.

Rise (verb): to move from a lower position, to a higher one; come or go up

1. *I watch the bread rise in the bowl before placing it in the oven.*

2. *I have worked my entire life to feel confident, to find recovery, it is my time to rise.*

I am Finding my way Rainbow Bagels
Adapted from Recipe by Ashlee Marie

Most people see the world in black and white, I see it in technicolor and I am finally becoming ok with that. Seeing my lens as a super power rather than my achilles heel has changed the way I see myself. I am not perfect, I never will be, I don't think I actually want to be, but I am finding my way.

Ingredients
- 2 cups warm water
- 1 tablespoon active dry yeast
- 2 tablespoons brown sugar
- 1 teaspoon salt
- 3 ½ cups flour
- 1 package of food dye

Equipment
- Stand mixer
- Parchment Paper
- Pot for boiling water
- Baking sheet

Instructions

For the first color:

1. Place the warm water, 1 tablespoon of sugar and yeast in a stand mixing bowl, let it sit for 10 minutes.

2. Add the rest of the sugar, salt and flour gradually (about ½ cup at a time).

3. Knead the dough until it has a bit of "bounce".

4. Add food dye to the dough.

5. Grease a bowl and place dough inside, refrigerate while you make the first color.

6. Repeat the steps for each color you want to make (recommend 5-6 colors).

7. Once the colors are done, bring the bowls out of the fridge and let rise until they double in size.

8. Stretch out dough (for each color) into a rectangle and place on parchment paper, repeat and layer each color.

9. Once all is layered, cut the dough in half so you have double the colors.

10. Cut a slice and roll into a 1 inch thick strip, twist and wrap around

your hand, let the dough overlap about two inches and make a circle shape.

11. Place dough on parchment paper and let rise for 20 minutes.
12. Preheat the oven to 375F.
13. Bring a pot of water to a boil.
14. Boil each bagel for about one minute then place on a parchment paper lined baking sheet.
15. Bake for 20 minutes.

Electricity

My Energy
Sparkles
Like a firecracker
A crackle
Almost audible
At this
Ungodly hour
A calling to create.
Dimming this light
Feels irresponsible
Like leaving a candle
To burn unattended
Till morning.

I don't know what to do
With this need to
Make something
At midnight.
Maybe
It's a need for more
To leave this world
A little better than I found it.
It hasn't always been kind to me.
But that has never left me with

Resentment
Only hope to
Make something new.
What to do
With this energy.
It runs through my blood
filling the well of passion
That lays within my soul
Nothing feels quite big enough to
honor this energy
I guess I have always believed
I was meant for more
Than what my mind could even imagine.
I wish I had a resolution for this
electric feeling
But sometimes
The best thing I can do is
Hold onto believing I will
Find a way to ignite
In a way that
Will be big enough
For what I was born to do.

Relief

Relief
Comes on Wednesdays at 6PM
When my therapist and I detangle the
anxious webs
I have woven throughout the week.
She helps me tease them apart
while I hold the fine tooth comb.

I am not scared anymore
We nurture the broken string.

Healing for me
Is not a solo act
It takes a guide to help
Process beyond myself.
I am learning the route out
Is what leads me back in.

Pieces

You are a mirror reflecting all of my broken
pieces
Back at me.
A beautiful mess
Torn apart and
Placed back together.
Pieces with sharp edges
And broken corners
Yet you want them all.

Fire Alarm

They say grief comes in waves
But I hardly feel like I'm on an adequate
surfboard.

My grief doesn't live in the ocean.
It feels so hot, it overtakes me.
And it's quick,
like fire.
A tight chest, swollen eyes,
The tears that fall
can't begin to extinguish
what's about to go up in flames.

Learning to self soothe through grief
When I can't trust the person inside
Makes it even more difficult to leave this
burning building.
The adrenaline may move my feet,
my arms may open the door
But my mind is stuck in the fire.
Grasping for lifelines, someone to help
Do this work with me?
Help me heal?

But I am in this fire,
alone.

The tears fall
Time starts to heal
The fire dissipates.

This time,
I rebuild
with fireproof drywall.
So, when my grief inevitably triggers the
fire alarm again
Even when my building goes up in flames
I will be left with a little
structure.

Not Alone

I wonder what it would be like when we told
you
You are not alone, you believed it.
I have been there,
Alone.
And just hearing those words
Are sometimes enough to pull back
The layer of rubble that coats the top of your
aloneness.

What if you felt it?
What I feel at 4PM
in my healing circle,
Would you believe it?
Would you know the feeling is temporary?
That you
Alone
Matter
That even below the rubble
We can see you
Because you alone
Are connected to us.

Watch Me Rise

I am living proof resilience exists.
I can name what has knocked me down
And I shine through what has pulled me
back up.
I am strong.
For the first time,
I might understand why,
I belong here
On Earth.
That even in my corner
I undoubtedly
make waves

Nurture the broken

I am in love and apparently I am easy to
love,
I cried when I heard that.

I was told once "I love you" was impossible
to say
To someone who I loved with all of me.
Impossible to love
Made it feel impossible to live
Because what is life without love?

My heart shattered when he ended it
But I put it back together.
My true partner heals it.
He nurtures the broken.
I find the glue,
I believe I am easy to love.

Inner Dialogue

I call myself a hypocrite
A liar, a fake
An inauthentic—
Stop.

I am not a hypocrite
I am navigating recovery
A journey that is far from
And may never be over.

I am not a liar
I practice what I preach.
I step into my recovery honestly
With no agenda
Or timeline
No roadmap
I do not lie,
Life is unfolding
In a way that will be true
To me.

I am not a fake
I don't claim to be anything

But imperfect. A human,
One that's figuring out how to navigate
The 71 billon dollar diet industry
With the body positivity movement
Or the body neutrality movement
Or the Body anything movement
All I do is think about my body.

I am authentic
I am not done
I will not let myself
Inaccurately slap a label
On a hand that just wants to be held
To be told I am doing great

I am not a hypocrite
I am growing and that includes steps
Back, forward and side
I do not claim to be anything but trying.

Magic

There is something about advocacy
That feels nothing short of magic.
My voice is my power.
My responsibility is healing.
I am changing the world.

Thank you so much for coming on this
journey with me!
Want to learn more about Bake it Till You
Make it LLC by Dayna Altman?

The Organization: Bake it Till You Make it
LLC is a community-based organization
dedicated to destigmatizing mental illness,
normalizing mental health conversation, and
promoting authentic healing and recovery.
Bake it Till You Make it LLC seeks to
connect people through food, making
"difficult conversation" more palatable,
natural, and—in turn—commonplace, by
using creativity, connection, and community.

Previous Work by Bake it Til You Make it
LLC includes:

Books:

- *Bake it Till You Make it: Breaking
  Bread, Building Resilience* (Award-
  Winning Cookbook, 2019): The first-
  of-its-kind mental health and

resilience cookbook that tells the inspirational and resilient stories of over forty people, from all different backgrounds, who have overcome major life challenges. Each story is accompanied by a baking recipe chosen by the contributor. The book features mental health resource pages, complete with a self-care guide and information on how to become a mental health ally. The book has since inspired a movement to destigmatize mental illness and create a space to encourage vulnerability and authenticity to connect us all.

- *Mix, Melt, Mend: Owning my Story & Finding my Freedom* (Memoir, 2020): The authentic account of the journey of Dayna Altman. Dayna, a mental health advocate, is the creator of Bake it Till You Make it LLC, which published the first-of-its-kind mental health and resilience cookbook, *Bake it Till You Make it:*

Breaking Bread, Building Resilience.
In *Mix, Melt, Mend*, Dayna tells her
own story in the framework of a cake
pop recipe.

- *A Unifying Blend: A compilation of
  recipes and stories to celebrate all
  that makes us Human:* A unique
  cookbook that uses baking to share
  the authentic and brave stories of
  over thirty individuals varying in
  age, background, and identity.
  Coupled with mental health resource
  pages, this book explores what it
  means to be unified by strength,
  struggle, resilience, and food. Step
  into the lives of the brave, feel
  inspired by their journeys, and learn
  about the importance of mental
  health (you might even find a new
  favorite recipe)!

Presentations

- Bake it Till You Make it: Live!: A
  one-hour program facilitated by

mental health activist and mental health cookbook author, Dayna Altman. Dayna tells the story of her mental health experience and the healing she has found through advocacy, specifically in creating the first-of-its-kind mental health and resilience cookbook, *Bake it Till You Make it: Breaking Bread, Building Resilience*. Dayna uniquely weaves her story through a demonstration as she bakes two recipes from her cookbook. Dayna uses ingredients as metaphors to guide her talk. She also brings up members of the audience to share pieces of their own stories as they work through the recipes together.

Community Initiatives

- Beyond Measure Bakery by Bake it Till You Make it LLC: On a mission to make mental health conversation a "piece of cake," Beyond Measure

Bakery combines boxes of baked goods and vetted resources to educate and empower the community to better understand mental health. This bakery believes in vulnerable conversation, an authentic lifestyle, and that sprinkles belong on everything.

- Beyond Measure: The Podcast: A project that explores authentic storytelling, purpose, and vulnerability with community leaders, local role models, and everyday individuals who share their journeys to finding "their worth is beyond measure." Inspired by Beyond Measure Bakery by Bake it Till You Make it LLC, this podcast is a space to explore meaning, motivation, and community along with a love of baked goods.
- Boston's Annual Bake it Till You Make it x Nailed it! Inspired by the hit Netflix show, this friendly baking and decorating competition is a

staple community event that brings together mental health resources, vulnerable storytelling and decorating challenges.

Ways to Get in Touch:

- Website: www.bakeittillyoumakeit.co
- Email: bakeitcookbook@gmail.com
- Social Media
  - Instagram: bakeittillyoumakeitllc
  - TikTok: bakeittillyoumakeitllc
  - Facebook: Bake it Till You Make it
  - YouTube: Bake it Till You Make it

Hope to hear from you!

About the Author:

Dayna Altman (She/her/hers) is an energetic
and dynamic entrepreneur, author, and
creator. The full force and sole operator of
Bake it Till You Make it LLC, Dayna
harvests her passion for mental health
advocacy by using food and baking to create
an authentic recipe for vulnerable
storytelling.

A dual graduate of Northeastern University and an active Boston community member, Dayna has experience both working in the mental health field and with youth-based non-profits. Currently, Dayna works at a national education non-profit, and in all other hours of the day, she pursues public speaking, writing poetry and cookbooks, documentary filmmaking, and exploring new ways to change the world using her own story. Her activism has been featured by MTV, Aerie, and at the White House alongside the Biden-Harris administraiton. Living with depression and OCD, as well as being in recovery from an eating disorder and sexual assault, Dayna Altman truly lives her message.

About the Illustrators:

Gabby Alvarez (she/they) is a mental health, food justice, and social justice advocate. As a senior in high school she strives to help those in her community rise above their struggles; whether this is through agricultural work at their job or at school as president of the Advocates for Social Justice Club. Gabby holds pride in being part of the LGBTQ+ community in addition to growing up in a Latinx household. Gabby hopes to pursue a career in social work and one day open her own non-profit organization.

Illustrator: Dark & Twisty Pretzels, Rainbow Bagels

Mekkailah Chourb (She/her/hers)is a senior at Lynn Vocational High School and studies in early education and care. Along her school life, Mekkailah takes pride in being apart of Skills USA and loves doing volunteer work. Currently, she works passionately alongside other youth and adults at the Food Project. During her free time, she loves to create and listen to music.

Illustrator: An Ode to All Things Bad for Me, Magical Thinking

Iwinosa Foster-Efosa (She/her/hers) is an African American illustrator who sleeps on the borders of reality and imagination; however that would be impossible as she would have to pay for housing and accommodation in both worlds. Iwinosa focuses on diverse illustrations and enjoys conveying deep feelings in her art as she feels representation and reliability matter. A lover of all things art, Iwinosa's additional interests include binge-watching Korean dramas, playing video games and being active through sports, especially paintball and at the arcade.

Illustrator: Homesick, Not a Role Model, Skin, Nineteen, Duality, Honor, Electricity, Relief

Elvira Tejada Lemus (He/They/She) is 17 years old, a high school senior. They enjoy taking opportunities to express themselves creatively whether it be painting, crocheting, writing, or playing music. On top of that they find joy when they're helping out their community either by volunteering or working at their job, The Food Project. The Food Project was a space for Elvira to learn about social justice, food justice, and to connect with themselves and the land. As graduation approaches, their next steps are heading off to college with a major in environmental studies & sustainability and overall just doing more of the little things that make them happy. <3

Illustrator: Sit Tight, The Invisible War, Freedom

Emily Barden is a Boston based amateur artist with a studio art education from UMass Amerherst. She works with an array of mediums and enjoys painting portraits of dogs. Find her on art Instagram account:

@emilybardenart or connect with her personally (also on IG): @emilybarden97

Illustrator: Stress Hives (Not a) Friend, Anxiety, Held Up

Leslie Barden is an amatuer artist from Hyde Park who enjoys working with a variety of mediums. She loves all things fitness, especially skiing and cycling, as well as baking. Leslie is passionate about bringing awareness to mental health, and enjoys when her passions can be used to support mental health efforts.

Illustrator: 100mg, Banana Bread, Gluten Free Bread, Sourdough Bread

Melody Gregory MS, is a Mental Health Counselor who aims to bring light-heartedness and humor to her work in order to support youth and families in an authentic and genuine way.

Illustrator: Nurture the Broken

George Gregory is currently working as an ABA therapist with children on the autism spectrum. Before this he held a career working in after school programs and child care settings across Massachusetts. He is currently exploring new pathways in order to use his experience within his community.

Illustrator: Not Alone

Allee DeFronzo

Allee DeFronzo (she/her/hers) is a young professional born and raised in Lynn Massachusetts. Allee is a graduate of Boston University and has used her background in science and math to educate youth in her home community of Lynn for the past ten years. Allee met Dayna through their time spent at the same youth based non profit and has been excited and honored to be part of the Bake it til you make it community that Dayna has built. Outside of her current job as a Product Owner, Allee enjoys spending time with family and friends, being outside, and traveling. She is passionate about social justice, education, and the environment.

Illustrator: Perception (exclusively for the Watch Me Rise Exhibit) , Pieces

Andy Wilson

Illustrator: Scattered, Starving

Kamryn Smith is from Southeastern Ohio. She is an Admissions Representative at University of Rio Grande. She enjoys reading, writing, and spending time with her cat Alfie. Her favorite form of self-expression is her wardrobe! "Reaching for Calm" is her first watercolor painting and was inspired by Dayna Altman's poem "Anxiety."

Illustrator: Anxiety, If ED Could Speak, Magic

Sam Rogers is a software developer at Mequilibrium, an organization based in resilience and helping people find wellness in the workplace. Outside of work, he loves all things music. In June 2022, he released his first EP: Hopeful Nostalgia by his musical persona, Sentin. He also enjoys spending time with his girlfriend (the author of this book), chosen family and biological family. Check out his music: www.sentinmusic.com

Illustrator: Fire Alarm

Sheryl Altman

Illustrator: Watch Me Rise

Tiffani

Illustrator: Crossroads

Brenna Stewart

Illustrator: Dedication

Jessica Webb

Illustrator: Perception

Jenna Altman

Illustrator: Silence

Laura McCoy

Illustrator: Lost and Found

Taryn B. Meadows

Illustrator: Inner Dialogue

CPSIA information can be obtained
at www.ICGtesting.com
Printed in the USA
LVHW070141160223
739523LV00006B/68